SOUND *Artistry*
INTERMEDIATE METHOD *for* FLUTE

PETER BOONSHAFT & CHRIS BERNOTAS

T0025117

in collaboration with

JULIETTA CURENTON

Thank you for making *Sound Artistry Intermediate Method for Flute* a part of your continued development as a musician. This book will help you progress toward becoming a more able and independent musician, focusing on both your technical and musical abilities. It offers material ranging from intermediate to advanced, making it valuable for musicians at various experience levels.

The many instrument-specific exercises in this book will help to support your personal improvement of techniques on your instrument, focusing on skills that may not always be addressed in an ensemble or in other repertoire. You will notice there are many performance and technique suggestions throughout the book. This wonderful advice has been provided by our renowned collaborative partners, as well as the many specialist teachers we worked with to create this book.

Sound Artistry Intermediate Method for Flute is organized into lessons that can be followed sequentially. As you progress through each lesson, it is a good idea to go back to previous lessons to reinforce concepts and skills, or just to enjoy performing the music. Exercises include Long Tones, Flexibility, Major and Minor Scales (all forms), Scale Studies, Arpeggio Studies, Chromatic Studies, Etudes, and Duets, as well as exercises that are focused on skills that are particular to your instrument. You will notice that many studies are clearly marked with dynamics, articulations, style, and tempo for you to practice those aspects of performance. Other studies are intentionally left for you to determine those aspects of your musical interpretation and performance. This book progresses through various meters and every key. Once a key has been introduced, previous keys are interspersed throughout for reinforcement and variety. In the back of this book you will also find expanded-range scale pages and a detailed fingering chart.

We wish you all the best as you continue to develop your musicianship, technique, and artistry!

~ Peter Boonshaft and Chris Bernotas

Julietta Curenton is Assistant Professor of Flute at Shenandoah Conservatory in Winchester, Virginia and the principal flutist of the acclaimed National Philharmonic. Ms. Curenton has also collaborated extensively with the Orpheus Chamber Orchestra, Imani Winds, The Ritz Chamber Players, Baltimore Symphony, and the National Symphony. She holds a BM from The Juilliard School; an MM from The Royal Northern College of Music and is currently completing a DMA from Stony Brook University.

Alfred

alfred.com

ISBN-10: 1-4706-6650-2
ISBN-13: 978-1-4706-6650-7

Instrument photos provided courtesy of Jupiter Band Instruments/KHS America

Lesson 1

1 LONG TONES

Slowly ♩= 60

2 LONG TONES: CHROMATIC

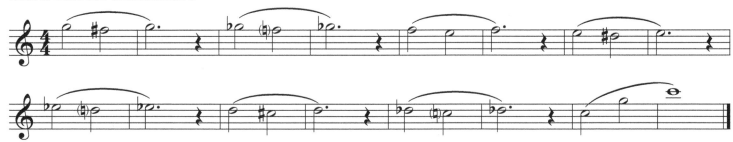

3 FLEXIBILITY—*This exercise requires a full, deep breath for proper air support with a fast air stream for the low register notes. If low notes are fully supported, then the extra air taken at the beginning of each phrase will help support the higher register notes.*

4 C MAJOR SCALE AND ARPEGGIO

5 C MAJOR SCALE STUDY

6 ARPEGGIO STUDY

7 ETUDE—*Play all etudes slowly with a steady tempo and good tone quality before speeding up. Always keep a good tone in mind and perform with musicality.*

Moderato ♩ = 100

8 ETUDE

Deliberately ♩ = 108

9 ETUDE—*Practice this etude with two-bar phrases and then four-bar phrases.*

Legato ♩ = 80

10 DUET

Majestically ♩ = 82

Lesson 2

11 **LONG TONES**

Slowly ♩ = 60

12 **A MINOR SCALE**

Natural   Harmonic

Melodic   Arpeggio

13 **A MINOR SCALE STUDY**

14 **ETUDE**

Moderately ♩ = 72

15 **ETUDE**

Pensively ♩ = 60

16 CHROMATIC SCALE

17 CHROMATIC SCALE ETUDE

Moderately ♩ = 88

18 ETUDE

Lightly ♪ = 120

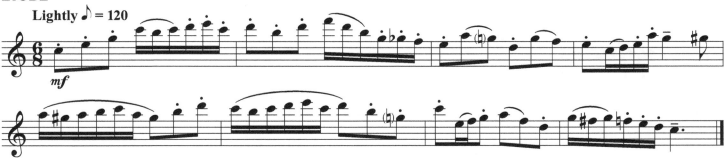

19 ETUDE—*After playing this etude as written, create or improvise a new ending for the last two measures.*

Moderately ♩ = 100

Lesson 3

20 LONG TONES

Slowly ♩ = 60

21 Bb FINGERING OPTIONS—*For this exercise, try using the alternate Bb (thumb) fingering, though you will need to use the long/regular Bb (1+1) fingering to accommodate the B naturals. It is good to have the flexibility and ability to use both the long/regular Bb and thumb Bb, in general.*

Allegro ♩ = 112

22 F MAJOR SCALE AND ARPEGGIO—*For all scale exercises that are written in octaves, practice each octave separately and then as a two-octave scale and arpeggio. Sing or hum these notes before playing them. Internalizing the pitch will help develop your aural skills.*

23 F MAJOR SCALE STUDY

24 ETUDE

Walking tempo ♩ = 104

25 ARPEGGIO STUDY—*Remember to always have proper posture, embouchure, and hand position to promote performing with a beautiful tone.*

Lesson 4

28 D MINOR SCALE

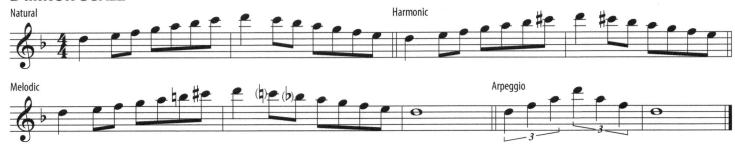

29 D MINOR SCALE STUDY

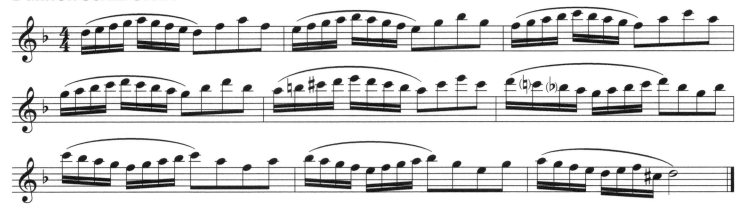

30 ETUDE

31 ETUDE

32 **DUET**—*Work towards matching each of the musical elements in this duet for a unified performance.*

33 **ETUDE**—*Play this etude with an eighth-note pulse until the rhythm is accurate. Then, transition to the dotted-quarter-note pulse.*

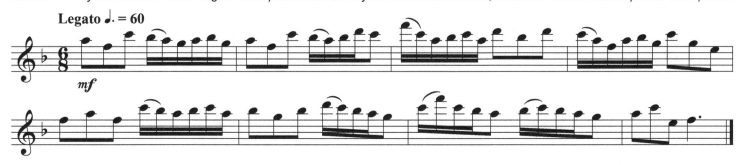

Lesson 5

34 ETUDE

Allegro ♩ = 120

35 ETUDE

Legato ♩ = 88

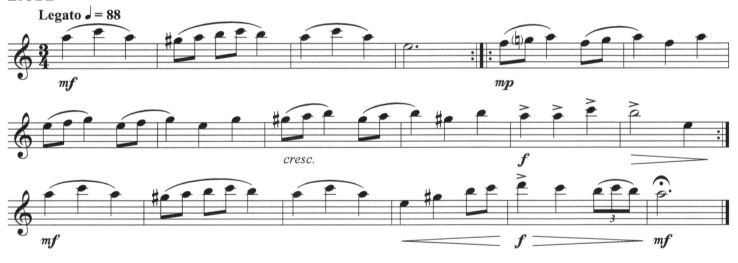

36 ETUDE

Evenly ♩ = 96

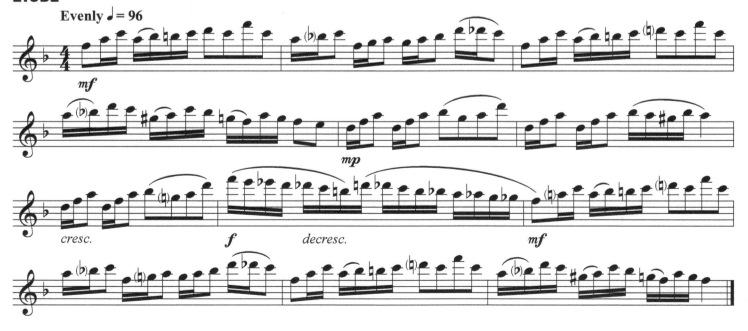

37 **ETUDE**

Stately ♩ = 98

38 **DUET**

Maestoso ♩ = 72

39 **ETUDE**

Cantabile ♩ = 72

Lesson 6

Every fingering on the flute can produce several other pitches simply by adjusting the embouchure and the direction of the air, as well as increasing the air speed. These are called **HARMONICS**. To produce harmonics in the example shown, use the fingering and set your embouchure to play the low D (called the fundamental). Then gradually increase the air speed as you adjust the embouchure and direction of air to make the higher harmonics sound. This can be done using any low note as the fundamental.

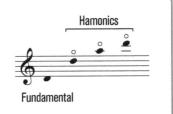

40 HARMONICS—*For notes that do not have the harmonic symbol, use standard fingerings.*

41 G MAJOR SCALE AND ARPEGGIO

42 G MAJOR SCALE STUDY—*Using manuscript paper or notation software, compose a new scale study that you think is even more challenging.*

43 OCTAVE SLURS—*Octave leaps are particularly challenging. Think about the position of your throat. First, play the low G to feel the placement of your throat. Then, play the high G. Notice how different they feel. Try the etude after you can identify the different throat positions. The trick is to keep your throat in the low position for the entire measure. The high notes will speak if you push faster air through the instrument, then slow down the air to return to the lower pitch.*

44 RANGE EXTENSION

45 **INTERVAL STUDY**—*Once you are comfortable with this as written, practice it an octave higher.*

46 **ETUDE**

Andantino ♩ = 80

47 **ETUDE**—*Practice this etude with two-bar phrases and then four-bar phrases.*

Dolce ♩ = 80

48 **ETUDE**

Moderately ♩ = 112

Lesson 7

49 **FLEXIBILITY**

50 **E MINOR SCALE**

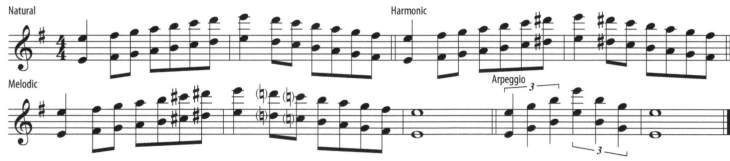

51 **E MINOR SCALE STUDY**—*For the high F♯s in this study, experiment with using the alternate fingering (including finger 5). See which fingering gives you better tone and intonation.*

52 **ETUDE**

53 **HARMONICS**—*For notes that do not have the harmonic symbol, use standard fingerings.*

54 ETUDE

55 ETUDE—*After successfully playing this etude, seek guidance from a teacher for ways you can refine your performance.*

56 ETUDE

Lesson 8

57 **FLEXIBILITY**

58 **B♭ MAJOR SCALE AND ARPEGGIO**

59 **B♭ MAJOR SCALE STUDY**

60 **ETUDE**—*If this exercise is not rhythmically even at the dotted-quarter-note pulse, try setting your metronome to the eighth-note pulse of ♪ = 180.*

61 **ETUDE**—*Be creative with the musicality of this etude by altering and adding your own dynamic markings.*

62 DUET

63 G MINOR SCALE

64 G MINOR SCALE STUDY

65 ETUDE—*Be sure that your tongue is as low (or forward) as possible for clear and pronounced attacks.*

Lesson 9

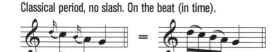

GRACE NOTES are ornaments that are performed before the beat or on the beat, depending on the musical time period, style, context, and notation. The last example below shows how unslashed grace notes would be performed in the Classical period. Listen to music from various historical periods and notice the different approaches to the performance of grace notes.

Most often performed before the beat | Classical period, no slash. On the beat (in time).

66 GRACE NOTES—*Play these grace notes just before the main note.*

67 ETUDE

68 ETUDE—*An appoggiatura is a grace note without a slash that is played on the beat. In this exercise, measures 1 and 5, as well as measures 3 and 7, would be played the same.*

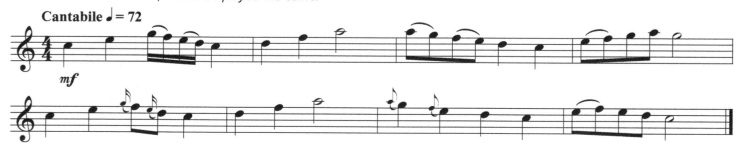

69 ETUDE

70 ETUDE

71 **ETUDE**

72 **ETUDE**—*Record your performance of this etude. Recognize the personal musical growth you have made from when you sight-read the piece. Think about the technical and musical ways your performance has improved. Do you hear a difference?*

73 **ETUDE**—*A tip for playing fast is to keep your fingers curved and close to the keys. If you can hear your keys click, your fingers are not close enough.*

Lesson 10

74 **LONG TONES**

75 **FLEXIBILITY**

76 **ETUDE**

77 **ETUDE**—*This etude requires great breath support. To take a deep breath, make an "O" shape with your lips and aim for the breath to be silent. The quieter the breath, the deeper the breath will be.*

78 CHROMATIC SCALE

79 CHROMATIC RANGE

80 MAJOR SCALE RANGE—*There are often many different fingerings for notes on the flute. You should learn the regular fingerings first, then integrate alternate fingerings where appropriate. For this exercise, after playing it with the regular high F♯ fingering (using finger 6), try using the alternate F♯ fingering. Which fingering sounds better?*

81 DUET   Andante ♩ = 108

Lesson 11

82 FLEXIBILITY

83 D MAJOR SCALE AND ARPEGGIO

84 D MAJOR SCALE STUDY

Moderately ♩ = 120

85 ETUDE

Adagio ♩ = 60

86 ETUDE—*When playing extremely fast passages moving between E and F♯, an alternate fingering may be used for the F♯ (including finger 5). After practicing this etude at the written tempo using the standard fingering, try increasing the speed using the alternate fingering. Regular F♯ has much better tone and intonation, so it is almost always the desired fingering, other than when trilling.*

Allegro ♩ = 90

continued on next page

87 **FINGER TWISTERS**—*Practice each twister slowly and increase the speed as you become more comfortable.*

88 **ETUDE**—*After performing this etude, discuss the various elements of the musical work with a peer or teacher.*

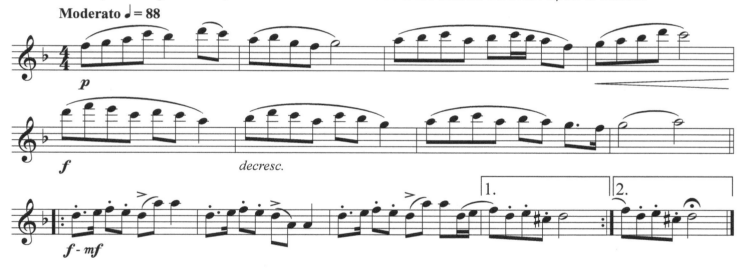

89 **ETUDE**—*This is a great etude to practice using your alternate B♭ (thumb) fingering. Remember that to play the high F♯ in measure 16 you will need to abandon that alternate thumb placement. Use the high G to transition to the regular thumb key. You can then switch back to the alternate B♭ (thumb) fingering for the remainder of the etude.*

Lesson 12

90 **FLEXIBILITY**

91 **B MINOR SCALE**

92 **FINGER TWISTERS**

93 **B MINOR SCALE STUDY**

94 **DUET**

A **TRILL** is an ornament that is performed by alternating rapidly between the written note and the next diatonic note above. Sometimes you will see a natural, sharp, or flat sign with a trill, which means to alternate between the written note and the next altered note. Always check the key signature. For these examples, use the regular fingering for the trill, except for E to F♯, where you would use the alternate F♯ (finger 5.)

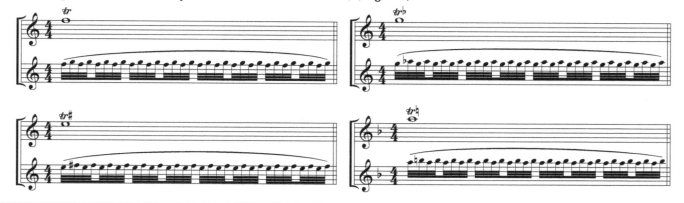

95 TRILLS—*Use your metronome to ensure an even and consistent rhythm.*

96 TRILLS—*Practice this exercise to ensure your trills are played evenly. Remember, trill fingerings rarely require you to trill more than two fingers at a time. If the trill fingering requires more than that, it is the wrong fingering. Once you are comfortable with this exercise as written, try playing it in cut time (♩ = 160).*

97 TRILLS—*Practice measures 1–5 at a slow tempo to reinforce muscle memory, gradually increasing the tempo. This exercise will help ensure that your trills are played evenly.*

98 ETUDE—*In Baroque and Classical music, trills must start from the note above. Make sure to use the original fingering for the first upper note, then use the alternate trill fingering within the trill. For example, measure 2 includes a C to D trill. Begin with the regular D fingering, then use the first trill key (D) for the remainder of the trill. Also, grace notes are often used at the end of a trill. This ornament is also known as a nachschläge.*

Lesson 13

99 FLEXIBILITY

100 E♭ MAJOR SCALE AND ARPEGGIO

101 E♭ MAJOR SCALE STUDY

102 ETUDE

103 ETUDE

104 **DUET**

28

Lesson 14

105 LONG TONES

106 FLEXIBILITY

107 C MINOR SCALE

108 C MINOR SCALE STUDY

109 ETUDE

110 DUET

111 ETUDE

112 DUET—*While playing duets, both performers must listen critically to evaluate and adjust intonation.*

Lesson 15

113 FLEXIBILITY

114 A MAJOR SCALE AND ARPEGGIO

115 A MAJOR SCALE STUDY

116 ETUDE

117 ETUDE

118 **LONG TONES**—*Playing a note while singing the same note may help improve your tone quality. Try playing the note, then singing the note, then singing while playing the note. Finally, play the note without singing. Do you hear a difference in the tone?*

119 **F♯ MINOR SCALE**

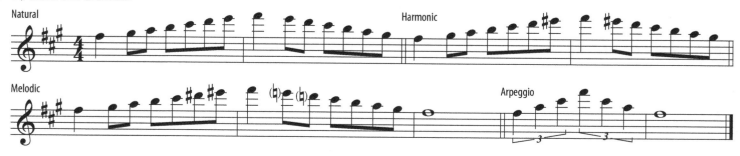

120 **F♯ MINOR SCALE STUDY**

121 **ETUDE**

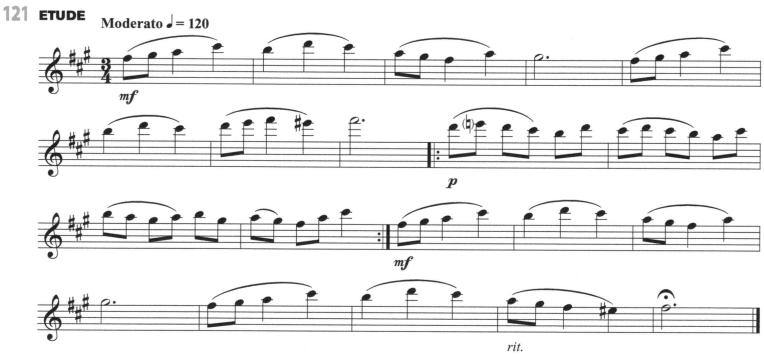

Lesson 16

122 **DUET**—*When playing ♪♫, remember to think of a sixteenth-note subdivision.*

123 **ETUDE**

124 **DUET**—*What musical elements in this duet make it engaging? How does the form contribute to the musical work?*

125 **ETUDE**

Lesson 17

126 FLEXIBILITY

127 Ab MAJOR SCALE AND ARPEGGIO

A **TURN** or **GRUPPETTO** is an ornament that involves playing the written note, followed by the note above it, returning to the original note, then playing the note below it, and finally ending on the original note.

128 Ab MAJOR SCALE STUDY

Adagio ♩ = 72

mf

129 Ab MAJOR SCALE STUDY

Moderato ♩ = 112

mf

130 ETUDE

Andante ♩ = 80

mf

continued on next page

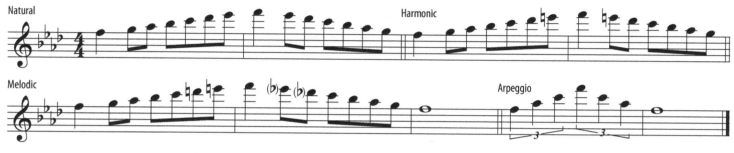

131 F MINOR SCALE

132 F MINOR SCALE STUDY

133 ETUDE

Lesson 18

134 OCTAVE SLURS

135 FLEXIBILITY

136 E MAJOR SCALE AND ARPEGGIO

137 E MAJOR SCALE STUDY

138 ETUDE

139 ETUDE

140 C# MINOR SCALES

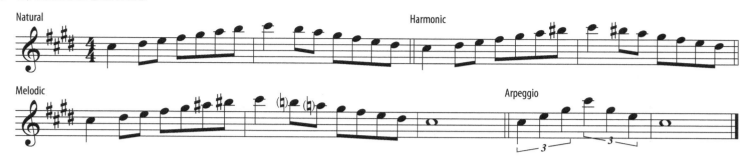

141 C# MINOR SCALE STUDY

142 ETUDE

143 DUET

Lesson 19

144 **FLEXIBILITY**

145 **ETUDE**

Allegro ♩ = 126

146 **ETUDE**

Legato ♩ = 72

147 **ETUDE**

Moderato ♩. = 60

148 **DUET**

149 **ETUDE**

150 **DUET**—*Use critical listening to improve the performance of all musical elements in this duet.*

Lesson 20

Fast, articulated passages often require the use of a technique called **DOUBLE TONGUING**. Double tonguing is a rapid articulation that alternates using the front/tip of the tongue and back of the tongue. Often, the syllables Ta Ka, Tu Ku, Da Ga, and Du Gu are used to help understand the tongue placement of this technique.

151 **DOUBLE TONGUING EXERCISE**—*For this exercise, practice four T articulations, then four K articulations, working toward making them sound the same. Then, practice double tonguing by alternating between T and K, still ensuring they sound the same. Use critical listening and experimentation to match the sound of each syllable.*

152 **DOUBLE TONGUING EXERCISE**—*As you become comfortable with this technique, increase the tempo and perform this exercise in cut time. Apply this pattern to other scales.*

153 **DOUBLE TONGUING EXERCISE**—*For a more fluid (connected) articulation, use the syllables Duh Guh or Du Gu, which will allow for a softer attack with less effort. You will also be able to play faster with these softer syllables. Notice your tongue placement will feel different from that of the tongue placement for the syllables Tu Ku. Here, you will not use the tip of your tongue to articulate. Instead, you should focus on the area of your tongue that is an inch away from the tip. Also, remember that your air speed helps lift your tongue, allowing you to play faster. If you find your tongue getting tired, your air speed is likely not fast enough to support the speed of your tongue.*

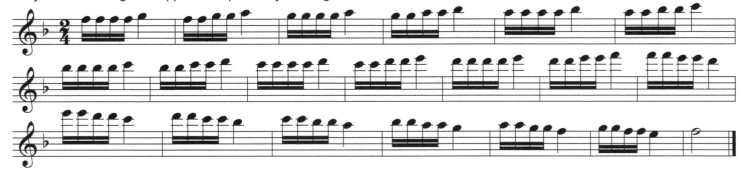

Fast, articulated passages in three-note groupings often require the use of a technique called **TRIPLE TONGUING**. Triple tonguing is a rapid articulation that alternates using the front/tip of the tongue and back of the tongue. Often, the syllables Ta Ta Ka or Duh Duh Guh are used to help understand the tongue placement of this technique. Use critical listening and experimentation to match the sound of each syllable.

154 TRIPLE TONGUING EXERCISE

155 TRIPLE TONGUING EXERCISE—*Experiment with using the tonguing patterns TTK and TKT to see which one is most comfortable and musical. Keep fast air speed to help losen the tongue.*

156 TRIPLE TONGUING EXERCISE—*Try playing this triple tonguing scale pattern in other keys.*

157 **ETUDE**—*Practice this with both single and double tonguing.*

Fanfare ♩ = 120

158 **ETUDE**—*Practice this with both single and triple tonguing.*

Majestic ♩ = 100

159 **DUET**

Majestic ♩ = 108

Lesson 21

160 FLEXIBILITY

161 Db MAJOR SCALE AND ARPEGGIO

162 ETUDE

163 ETUDE

164 Bb MINOR SCALES

165 ETUDE

Lesson 22

166 LONG TONES

167 B MAJOR SCALE AND ARPEGGIO

168 ETUDE

169 ETUDE

170 A♭ MINOR SCALE *(enharmonic spelling of G♯ minor)*

171 ETUDE *(enharmonic spelling of G♯ minor)*

Major Scales

C MAJOR

F MAJOR

B♭ MAJOR

E♭ MAJOR

A♭ MAJOR

D♭ MAJOR

G♭ MAJOR

C♭ MAJOR

G MAJOR

D MAJOR

A MAJOR

E MAJOR

B MAJOR

F♯ MAJOR

C♯ MAJOR

Minor Scales

A MINOR

Natural · Harmonic · Melodic

D MINOR

Natural · Harmonic · Melodic

G MINOR

Natural · Harmonic · Melodic

C MINOR

Natural · Harmonic · Melodic

Flute Fingering Chart

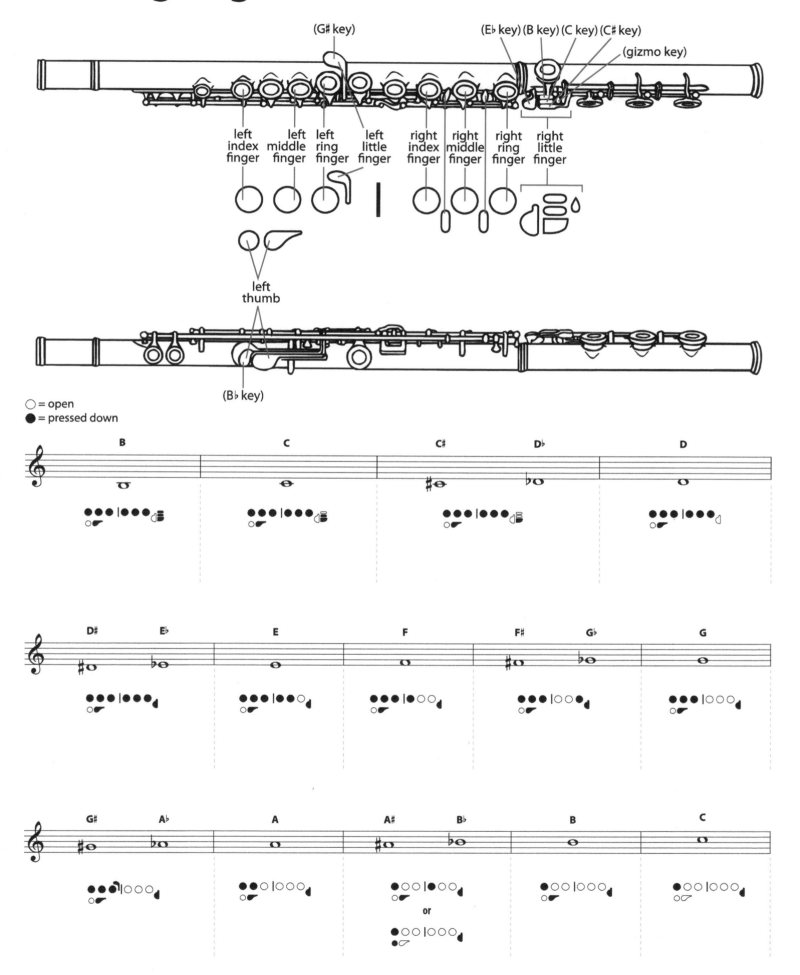

48

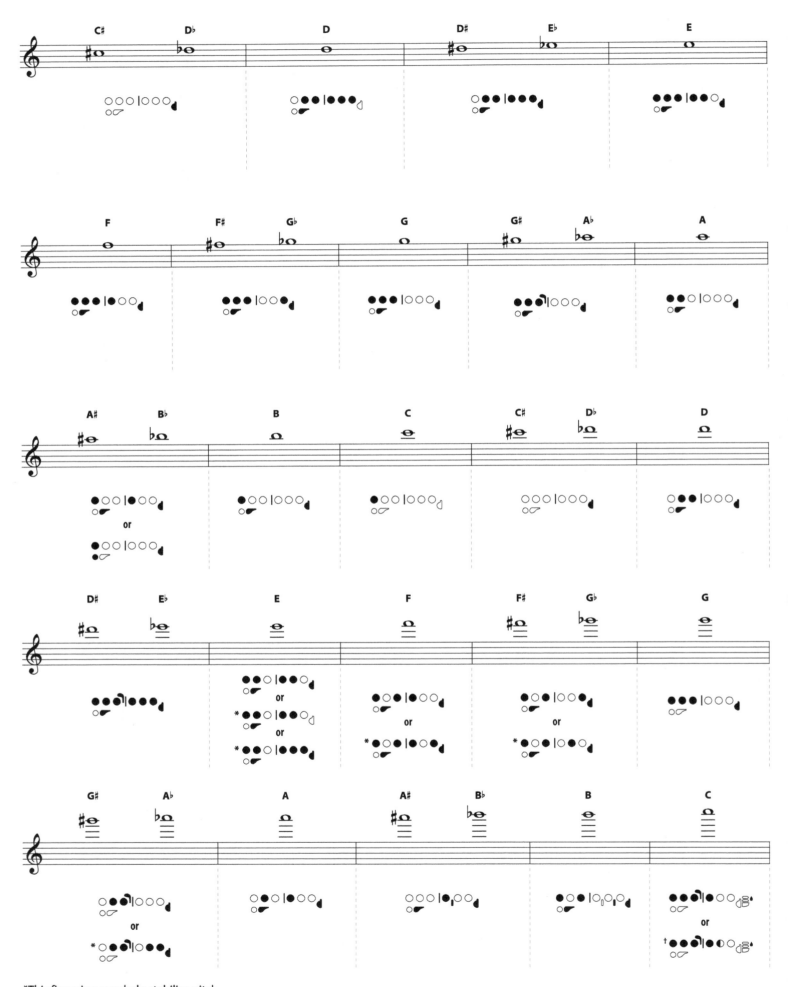

*This fingering may help stabilize pitch.
†This fingering is for open-hole flutes only.